STARTING OUT

CRANES

MEG GREVE

CREATIVE EDUCATION • CREATIVE PAPERBACKS

I SEE A CRANE.

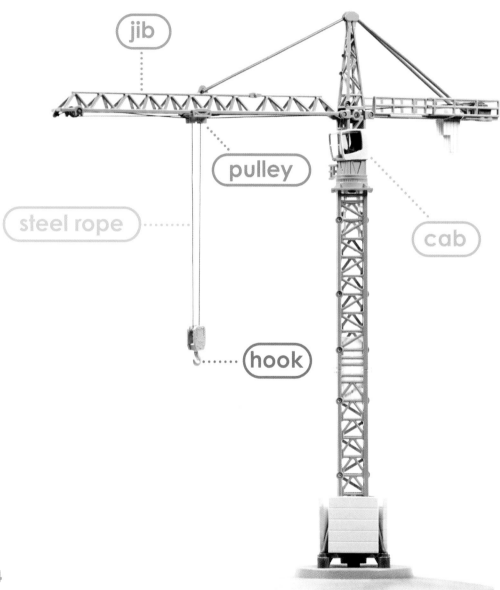

jib

pulley

steel rope

cab

hook

A crane's jib
is like a
giant arm.

The crane has a heavy
load on its hooks.

The driver makes the crane do the work.
The <u>steel</u> ropes move up.
The load lifts.

Cranes lift, move, **and** place. Cranes by the water load and unload ships.

A crane on a
ship helps build
a bridge.

I see a

<u>skycrane</u>.

Some cranes can fly. They do work from high in the air.

MAKE A
NOISE

WHIRR!

RRRRR!

Can you make the sounds
of a crane?

Listen to these sounds:

https://www.youtube.com
/watch?v=I6H8XJ7TLN4

Now it is
your turn!

CRANE WORDS

bridge: a structure built over something, such as a river, so people can cross

load: something that must be carried

skycrane: a special helicopter that can lift heavy things

steel: a very strong metal

READING CORNER

Mitton, Tony. *Amazing Machines: Colossal Cranes*. New York: Kingfisher, 2021.

Van Wright, Cornelius. *The Little Red Crane*. Cambridge, Mass.: Star Bright Books, 2020.

Zimmerman, Andrea. *Crane Jane! (Big Jobs, Bold Women)*. New York: Holiday House, 2023.

INDEX

PUBLISHED BY CREATIVE EDUCATION AND CREATIVE PAPERBACKS
P.O. Box 227, Mankato, Minnesota 56002
Creative Education and Creative Paperbacks
are imprints of The Creative Company
www.thecreativecompany.us

LIBRARY OF CONGRESS CATALOGING-IN-PUBLICATION DATA
Names: Greve, Meg, author.
Title: Cranes / by Meg Greve.
Description: Mankato, Minnesota : Creative Education and Creative Paperbacks, [2025] | Series: Starting out | Includes bibliographical references and index. | Audience: Ages 4-7 | Audience: Grades K-1 | Summary: "Construction cranes will introduce budding book learners to a noisy, colorful world with this new Starting Out title. Colorful photos, labeled diagrams, 'Make a Noise' section, glossary, and more ignite a passion for learning"-- Provided by publisher.
Identifiers: LCCN 2023059441 (print) | LCCN 2023059442 (ebook) | ISBN 9798889891697 (library binding) | ISBN 9781682775547 (paperback) | ISBN 9798889891819 (ebook)
Subjects: LCSH: Cranes, derricks, etc.--Juvenile literature. | Hoisting machinery--Juvenile literature. | CYAC: Cranes, derricks, etc. | Hoisting machinery. | LCGFT: Instructional and educational works.
Classification: LCC TJ1363 .G786 2025 (print) | LCC TJ1363 (ebook) | DDC 621.8/73--dc23/eng/20240129
LC record available at https://lccn.loc.gov/2023059441
LC ebook record available at https://lccn.loc.gov/2023059442

DESIGN AND PRODUCTION
Design by Rhea Magaro and Jennifer Bowers
Production by Beeline Media and Design
Art direction by Tom Morgan
Printed in the United States of America

PHOTOGRAPHS by Alamy (Jon Davison, David Gowans), Shutterstock (Potapov Alexander, freestore 839, karelnoppe, Nikolai Tsvetkov, Engineer studio, AlyoshinE, Oleksii Sidorov, Sven Hansche, Yuriy Shurchkov, Bohbeh, Suwin66)